SPIRITUAL
INTELLIGENCE

OKEY ONUZO

Spiritual Intelligence

Copyright© 2020, Okey Onuzo

ISBN: 978-1-880608-12-8

FIRST EDITION

TABLE OF CONTENTS

ACKNOWLEDGEMENTS

Yemisi Abegunde who transcribed the message preached at the City of David Church in Lagos, Nigeria.

Pastor Idowu Iluyomade who sent me the manuscript and encouraged me to publish the book.

Nneka Okonkwo who worked on the manuscript and positioned it for publication.

Over and above all, the Holy Spirit of God who gave the Word and set up the company that published it.

INTRODUCTION

I must give credit to God and the City of David, Victoria Island Parish of the Redeemed Christian Church of God, led by Pastors Idowu and Siju Iluyomade for the reality of this book. Some years ago, not sure which year to be precise, I did a series of teachings at the City of David that bordered on Spiritual Intelligence.

One day, I received a transcript of the message through the mail from Pastor Idowu with an encouraging note that a member transcribed it because she felt it should be a book. I was too busy then to address it. But suddenly, Covid-19 came along with its enforced lockdown, and what was not possible before became possible. Meetings all became Zoom meetings and we suddenly realized how much time we spent commuting to the venue of meetings.

Spiritual Intelligence is another name for the communion of the Holy Spirit that drives, directs and empowers us to glorify God on the earth in and through our lives. I gave my life to Christ through spiritual intelligence. It was the Holy Spirit of God who whispered to me that fateful day on June 28th, 1970 while going away from the venue of an invitational outreach meeting, that giving my life to Christ is what I should do. That voice and I have travelled together for close on fifty years. This makes spiritual intelligence a great part of my life. It made tough decisions look simple and easy because I had the Word that pointed in which direction I should be going.

Everybody needs spiritual intelligence for a thousand and one reasons. The more readily available it is to us, the easier our life's journey will be. My prayer is that the Holy Spirit will quicken every reader to embrace it or to go deeper still in it for the glory of God in us and through us, in Jesus' name, Amen.

Dr. Okey Onuzo

July' 2020

CHAPTER 1

You Need Spiritual Intelligence

Life is full of treacherous events. It is a common saying that things are often not what they seem to be, '*All that glitters is not gold*'. How can you avert a looming tragedy? How can you tell a friend from an enemy? This can only be possible when you get advice from someone with the expertise you lack, one who is reliably informed.

The Oxford Learner's Dictionary defines intelligence as:

1. the ability to learn, understand and think logically about things, and do this well

2. secret information collected, for example, about a foreign country, especially one that is an enemy; the people who collect this information

· intelligence reports
· the Central Intelligence Agency
·intelligence sources (= people who give this information)
· the head of military intelligence

We are more concerned with the second definition, which has some military undertone.

The bombing of the World Trade Centre in the United States of America by Islamic extremists on September 11, 2001, was described as a result of failed intelligence. And when the December 25, 2009 bomber, Umar Farouk Abdulmutallab, landed in America, it was also considered a failed intelligence. By implication, the intelligence departments like the Federal Bureau for Investigation (FBI) and the Central

Intelligence Agency (CIA) did not have sufficient insight into their enemies' plans. As a result, America was dealt deadly blows on one occasion. The essence of intelligence is that you have the necessary information for strategic decision making. This means that intelligence is used to prevent bad things from happening, and when you get it, you are always one step ahead.

However, in life, certain information is accessible only to divine intelligence and cannot be gotten by human intellect. This is why everybody needs spiritual intelligence, including the government, private organizations, and individuals. You want to know what the enemy is planning against you and then act based on that inside information. This inside information, we often refer to as revelation, a divine supernatural disclosure of spiritual plan soon to be manifested in the natural realm. The government of ancient Egypt was saved from being caught unawares by famine when the Pharaoh of Egypt had a mysterious dream. God revealed its interpretation to Joseph, and so averted a colossal disaster. No human conceived strategy could have prepared the world for what was coming without the operation of spiritual intelligence in Joseph's life and, consequently, in Egypt's corridors of power (Genesis 41).

One day, our Lord Jesus told Peter that the devil had asked for permission to sift him like wheat and that the permission had been granted. He said to Peter, "To avert catastrophic destruction of your faith, I have prayed for you that your faith in Me and God will survive when it is all over.

"And the Lord said, "Simon, Simon! Indeed, Satan has asked for you, that he may sift you as wheat. But I have prayed for you, that your faith should not fail; and when you have returned to Me, strengthen your brethren."

- Luke 22: 31- 32 (NKJV)

The Purpose of Spiritual Intelligence

One of the greatest tragedies that can happen to a person is to receive intelligence and still allow the mischief to happen. When Boko Haram, an Islamic extremist terrorist group in Northern Nigeria, claimed they bombed the United Nations' (UN) building on Friday, August 26, 2011, Nigerian intelligence agencies disclosed that there had been intelligence reports that such a plan was in the offing. Despite that intelligence, the group succeeded in its evil plan. As it is in the natural, so it is in the spiritual.

1. Intelligence is always to ensure prevention. We use intelligence information to avert disasters and tragedies.

2. We also use intelligence information to seize opportunities in life and key into a fruitful season of our lives.

Often, when I'm listening to testimonies of how people were delivered here and there, the Holy Spirit always says to me, *"Those are wonderful testimonies, but they are all one step behind."* It is a marvel that God delivered me from the disaster that occurred here. The question I should ask myself is, 'Why was I there in the first place?'

I can never forget, and it's a true story - A man was on holiday and driving with his family. He went into a petrol station to fill his tank when the Spirit of God whispered to him: *"When you finish buying that gas, wait five minutes before continuing on your journey."*

So, he finished buying the gas, and he said to himself, "What will I be doing here for the next five minutes? Isn't that crazy?"

To him, sitting, waiting, and doing nothing at the filling station for five minutes was unreasonable, so he drove out. Two minutes later, a drunken driver hit him, and he was paralyzed from the neck down. Yes, everybody needs intelligence. You and I need information from spiritual intelligence now and again for protection. God wants to prevent things that you and I cannot foresee. The world is complicated and often in a hurry, and it might just take the right information, a little pause here, a little delay there, to keep us away for the danger to pass.

Spiritual Intelligence is for Those Wired to Receive It

In Matthew 2, the Bible says that wise men came from the East to Jerusalem and asked for the newborn King of the Jews. They had seen His star in the sky and had come to worship Him. When they came to Herod the king, he called for the religious leaders, the High Priest, the theologians, and the astrologers; and he asked them if they knew where the King of the Jews was to be born. They said, "*In Bethlehem Judea, for the prophets of old had prophesied about it.*"

Here, we see the difference between knowledge and intelligence. The religious leaders knew that the King would be born in Bethlehem, but when the birth itself occurred, they did not know. Instead, the information reached the wise men coming from the East, the shepherds close to Bethlehem, Simeon the saint, and Anna the prophetess. Spiritual intelligence is not always universally accessible. It is for those who are tuned in and restricted to those wired to receive such information.

King Herod called the wise men and said to them: "Go to Bethlehem and search for the newborn King and come back and tell me so that I can also go there and worship Him." (Matthew 2:7-8) Meanwhile, his utterance was different from his intention. Through his subsequent action detailed in Matthew Chapter 2, we learn that he had murderous plans. In a dream, Joseph, the husband of Mary, received warning of Herod's murderous intentions. God instructed him to escape the impending threat by relocating from the area that fell under King Herod's jurisdiction. This is a classic story that reveals the indispensability of spiritual intelligence. People may be telling you one thing while they are planning and plotting to undermine you completely. With spiritual intelligence, you can stay one step ahead of the devil's plots to lead you to sin and evil and so undermine your spiritual authority.

Spiritual Intelligence is Always Accurate

Joseph's response is quite remarkable and instructive. He did not doubt his spiritual intelligence. He did not have to send to Herod's courts to ascertain whether he had such murderous intentions. His information was dead on the mark as events subsequently proved when King Herod sent and murdered all the children from age two and under, in an attempt to kill our Lord and Saviour Jesus Christ.

We must avoid foolishness after we have received spiritual intelligence. In addition to revealing Herod's intention, spiritual intelligence prescribed what Joseph should do to avert the danger: *"Carry the baby and the mother and escape into Egypt."* There was already a prophetic word from the prophet Hosea, concerning that in the Bible. Hosea 11:1 was representative of what was about to happen to Joseph and Mary.

Now when they had departed, behold, an angel of the Lord appeared to Joseph in a dream, saying, "Arise, take the young Child and His mother, flee to Egypt, and stay there until I bring you word; for Herod will seek the young Child to destroy Him."

When he arose, he took the young Child and His mother by night and departed for Egypt, and was there until the death of Herod, that it might be fulfilled which was spoken by the

Lord through the prophet, saying, "Out of Egypt I called My Son."

> *- Matthew 2:13-15 (NKJV)*

When Israel was a child, I loved him, And out of Egypt I called My son.

> *- Hosea 11:1 (NKJV)*

Joseph's dream also served to key him and his family into this word of prophecy. It would have been foolish of Joseph to have said that if only he could pray fervently, the danger would be averted. This is the nature of foolishness. The Lord God Almighty, who would answer the prayer, had sent intelligence to instruct Joseph on what he needed to do to avert danger. Spiritual intelligence always speaks clearly and accurately about a situation on hand with warnings and instructions on preventing harm and danger. What we must always remember about Matthew 18:18 is that what a believer binds on earth will be bound in heaven.

Assuredly, I say to you, whatever you bind on earth will be bound in heaven, and whatever you loose on earth will be loosed in heaven.

- Matthew 18:18 (NKJV)

This tells us that the real binding takes place in heaven, not on earth. So when heaven sends us warnings and instructions, we would be foolish to ignore them. Opting to follow a preset notion of ways to respond to such situations will lead to tragedy, failure, and defeat.

Some years ago, a pastor in Ibadan in Nigeria told me that a certain gentleman was about to wed a lady. He and other brethren in the church received spiritual intelligence that the lady was not his wife and that he would not have the inner resources to weather the challenges that would emerge in the marriage. The young man defiantly responded that whatever would emerge would always bow to the pressure of prayer and fasting. People who ignore spiritual intelligence fall into a ditch. Its true value is that it serves to lead us beside still waters to refresh and restore our souls.

Spiritual Intelligence is for Stress Reduction

One day, I needed to go to Apapa Quays from Surulere, where I lived. I planned to return to my workplace at the Lagos University Teaching Hospital (LUTH) within an hour. So, I asked God what route to take to make it back to my office on time as I had a clinic that started at 9 am. He said that I should drive through Western Avenue. In man's logical fashion, I told God that there would be traffic congestion on that route at 8 am given the system of odd and even car number regulation that was subsisting: And He said to me, "*If you knew the way, why did you ask Me?*"

Spiritual intelligence overrides logic, so I drove through Western Avenue. Surprisingly, there was a free flow of traffic on that route and I was back at LUTH for my clinic at 9 am just like I prayed. Spiritual intelligence is also to reduce stress and make life easier for us.

Spiritual Intelligence is Borne of Love

Ninety-nine percent of the time, our God is preventive, and that's why our Lord Jesus taught us to pray in this order: *'And lead us not into temptation'* before *'Deliver us from evil'*. *"Lead us not"* – God wants us to avoid the matter altogether rather than get into it and have to be delivered from it. You know when you are not *"led into temptation"*, you don't have to be *"delivered from evil"*. If not, by the time heaven is delivering you and me from evil, we are already one step behind. That is because we've entered the problem and now have to be delivered.

Years ago, I went to the Ikoyi Club in Lagos to play squash, and when I finished, I was driving home, and my children were with a family friend at Ilupeju, a Lagos suburb. The Spirit of God said to me, *"Before you go home, go and check whether the children have gone home."* This incident was before the advent of the mobile phone, so I couldn't call my wife to verify. I thought to myself, "My wife is at home, there are drivers…, no way will the children still be there." I concluded that my wife must have sent one of the drivers to bring them home, but God said to me, *"But you are not sure of that, so, would you rather go home and come out again? Just go and check."*

I was arguing, and I said, "Lord, there is no way these children will still be there," and He kept saying, *"But you're not sure. There is no way you can be sure. So, why don't you just stop there?"*

I said, "Okay, Lord."

I drove to my friend's place and blared the horn without coming out of my car. Someone parted the curtains, and I asked: "Are they gone?"

"Yes, they are gone," came the response.

I said, "Lord, I told you there's no way they would still be here."

I didn't spend one minute at my friend's place, but then, as I drove away, I fell into a culvert. Something was missing from the channel over the gutter on the road, and I didn't realize it. Therefore, I fell into an open drain. It took me another fifteen minutes to find some help to get my car out of it. I drove home, not understanding what had happened, only to learn the next day that there had been an armed robbery melee at the Maryland junction right about the time I experienced those delays and diversions from the Lord. It was amazing.

We need to learn that God is preventive and that He will do everything to keep us from running into trouble. That's why I tell you that spiritual intelligence is out of love. Our Father in heaven would prefer to prevent stress and crisis for us than deliver us from it.

God always comes first. The reason why we begin with the spiritual is that the Bible says in Genesis 1:1 that "In the beginning God"... and our Lord Jesus told us in John 4:24 that *"God is spirit and they that worship Him must worship Him in spirit and truth."* Spiritual intelligence is essential because we need quite a bit of information to fulfill our calling here on earth. Without precise information and guidance from our Creator, we will be unable to follow His perfect plans.

For we are His workmanship, created in Christ Jesus unto good works, which God hath before ordained that we should walk in them.

- Ephesians 2:10 (KJV)

A preacher said, and I believe it, that after Christians are dead and gone to heaven, the angels who welcome us will take us on a tour of our lives. We will see two lines in some parts of our journey; and one line in some other regions. Two will mean that you were not running God's program, and one line would suggest that what you were doing coincided with what God wanted you to do. Two paths would mean that God had something else He wanted us to do, but we did our own thing. The Bible tells us in Ecclesiastes 3:14 that whatsoever God does is forever. What does that mean?

It means that when you and I follow the guidance of the Holy Spirit, His lead, and intelligence, our every move will conform in time to God's program for us in eternity. The things we do and say become the things God wants us to do and say. And that kind of immortalizes those things long after we are dead and gone. The wonder of the life that Christ lived on the earth is that He came to the earth and in three and a half years only, He completed the work that is to last for all time into eternity. It is amazing. I have always been fascinated by that.

He gave us a secret to that, though. He said, "Even the words that you hear Me speak are not My words." He said, "As I hear!" In other words, our Lord Jesus said, "I'm constantly transmitting to you the mind of the Father, the thoughts of the Father, the plans of the Father," and that is why He could live here for three and a half years and leave something that is indestructible. And the only way that could have been possible was that our Lord followed God's plans in detail.

CHAPTER 2

Spiritual Intelligence and Decision Making

"The gates of history turn on small hinges,
and so do people's lives."
- Thomas S. Monson

Decisions determine destiny. Quite often, momentary choices have a life-defining impact, which some never recover from in certain cases. When I was an undergraduate and in my second year at Medical School, my friends and I had gotten the baptism of the Holy Spirit. In those days, it was all new. There was so much excitement, and we were ministering everywhere, preaching, and traveling. Then, we got to the first year, Clinical, and we were still preaching and traveling, oblivious to the danger ahead of us. We would return home excited and rejoicing and spend hours talking about our exploits. We rarely slept till around 3.am. We were all so thrilled. By sixty-five days to the 'Part Two MB' exams, I got intelligence that we all failed.

So, I called my traveling companions and said to them, "Hey, there is a problem ahead, o!" From that day onwards, I didn't attend fellowship again — O yes, because the message said: '*Go on like this, and you will surely fail.*'

I knew that not adhering to divine revelation would be irresponsible, and I stopped and faced my books. I started to read at 7 am and did not stop till 11 pm. Some of my colleagues continued to travel and preach, and some consequently failed!

When we make life decisions, we make them from three perspectives. We have to consider:

1. The past because every decision that we make has an input that relates to the past.

2. The present because we live in the present.

3. The future because our aspirations mature in our tomorrow

Nobody has exhaustive knowledge. There is no way I can have thorough and complete knowledge about the past; neither can I have thorough knowledge about the present, but you and I know that we have no clue about the future. Nobody lives in the future now. There is only one person that can tell the future with certainty, and who is that? — God.

That's why we speak about Spiritual Intelligence.

Protection from Erroneous Conclusions

Decisions are conclusions made after the consideration of options laid before you. The value of spiritual intelligence is that God out of His bounteous grace and mercy, gives us a far off knowledge now so that we can live preventively at the end of the day. People who ignore spiritual intelligence fall into the ditch. They make all kinds of errors. They have all kinds of regrets, and after a few experiences like this, you learn that the basis of spiritual intelligence is love because the Father does not want evil, or crisis or disappointment to happen to you. That's why He goes out of His way to inform us. Spiritual intelligence is so relevant when we relate with people; when we have to take positions; when we have to execute projects.

Some time ago, my wife and I watched on the news; a national security chief publicly lambasted another senior ranking colleague of his for failing to produce a paper on how they would transform the force. Everybody thought, "This is new!"

There is crime everywhere, and we were saying, "Oh, this is wonderful. It is a welcome development." However, his continuing actions reported in the news showed that all he did was politically motivated.

You could support somebody who talks tough and in the public's interest, yet whose motives are not pure. You don't know why they are doing it. Only God can begin to reveal all these things so that you don't get yourself in a mess. You don't take positions that are not tenable when you know what the facts are. The Lord may not necessarily tell you what the circumstances are, but He will tell you: "*Don't get involved.*" You may not know why He said don't get involved, but when the facts come to light, you'll say: "Wow! These people would have made a total fool of me!"

Protection from Danger

During the World Trade Centre collapse in America, so many Christians had all kinds of stimuli and promptings that made them escape the tragedy. A man who worked in that building said that he normally left for work early, but he was delayed on that particular day. By the time he arrived for work, the building had collapsed. A pastor told me that after their Friday prayer meeting in a Staten Island Church, when everybody had dispersed and gone home, he felt an overwhelming urge to lay hands on all the auditorium seats and pray that God would preserve every member of the local assembly.

Meanwhile, he did not know what was coming, and quite a number of his church members worked in that building. Even his wife worked close to the building. Well, the bombing occurred on a Tuesday, and none of his church members was involved. The facts below reveal the gruesome tragedy when the 110 storey building fell.

"2,753 people died at the World Trade Center (WTC) site in Lower Manhattan when hijacked American Airlines Flight 11 and United Airlines Flight 175 were deliberately crashed into the building or as an outcome of the crashes."

- (Source: CNN.com)

Brethren, it is impossible to live successfully and to be safe without intelligence.

When your testimonies come a step or two behind God's actual plan and will, it shows that you did not get instructions from Him before proceeding. God is preventive, and you don't have to get to the point of deliverance, because the Scripture says '*and lead us not into temptation,*' but if you miss that, then the next one is applicable which says '*deliver us from all evil.*' The prayer, *lead us not,* is preventive, and you cannot live a preventive life without intelligence so that where ever you find yourself, you are confident that you are covered.

There was a time I wanted to travel to the UK, but I did not have the actual date to make the trip. I asked God about the trip, and He said to me, '*February 18, British Airways.*' In those days, I routinely did not fly British Airways. When I arrived at my travel agent's to arrange the flight, he said to me, "Doctor, you don't normally travel with British Airways. What is the matter?"

I said, "Yes, I know, but this time around, it must be British Airways."

On February 18, I flew with British Airways. When we got to Gatwick airport in London, the wind was gusting so much that the plane could not land. The people on board were panicking. However, what kept me calm was that it was February 18, and it was British Airways. Perhaps, if I had flown Swiss Air or any other airline, I would have been shaking too, but I was as calm as the ocean on a sunny day because I was walking in line with God's instructions. The plane could not land in London, alright, but the pilot took us to Manchester and landed us safely. Every Christian should take full advantage of the communion we have with the Holy Spirit as we travel the earth. The Bible tells us that the Holy Spirit searches God's mind to extract the vital information we need to make life's decisions on earth. He communicates the information to our quickened human spirit and so to us (1 Corinthians 2:9-12). This is how we can obtain heaven's approval or disapproval for whatever we want to do, all for our benefit.

Designed to Simplify Complexity

We find in the Book of 1st Samuel the story of a man who had the privilege to anoint two kings in his lifetime. The first time, he anointed Saul king. Before that time, there was no king in Israel. There was no such tradition. When a king dies, they'll say, 'Go to the royal family;' there was no royal family in Israel before this time. Israel had never had a king, but when they began to agitate, the question was: Who will Samuel anoint king?

If it were today, you'd see a lot of people lobbying, going to visit the prophet, taking care of him, taking him out to dinner, and sending him some goats and chickens in a bid to position themselves for favors. However, the Bible says that God spoke to Samuel in his ear one day and said, "*By this time tomorrow, I will send you the man you will anoint as king over Israel."* This information made Samuel's job easy.

Spiritual intelligence is designed to simplify things for us that are normally complicated. The all-knowing God gives the required information for you and me to make a decision that lies in the future now and do it with confidence and certainty. You'd watch a few years down the line and see how that decision was so dead on the mark because you received help from the all-knowing God.

We must get accustomed to making spiritually intelligent decisions. In Psalm 73:24, the psalmist said of the Lord:

"You will guide me with Your counsel."

That counsel is what spiritual intelligence is all about. It derives from the fact that our past, present, and future are always before God. Such revelatory intelligence helps to guide us through the minefield that is life on earth. We will avert all forms of unnecessary dangers and arrive at the shores of eternity with our joy, love for God, and faith intact. In Psalm 16:7, the psalmist said he would bless the Lord, who gives him counsel. God used to instruct him at night, so his day could be ordered in peace and safety.

It Is Not Based On Physical Senses

A lot of people think that life is random. No, the universe God made is well ordered from our knowledge of science, particularly molecular biology, so how will the spiritual life from which it is derived be so disordered? God orders everything, and that's why we need to follow what God says to us carefully.

2The Spirit of the Lord shall rest upon Him,
 The Spirit of wisdom and understanding,
 The Spirit of counsel and might,
 The Spirit of knowledge and of the fear of the Lord.

3His delight is in the fear of the Lord,
And He shall not judge by the sight of His eyes,
Nor decide by the hearing of His ears;

- Isaiah 11:2-3 (NKJV)

In other words, the judgment will go beyond the senses.

It would have ruined the day if Samuel, the kingmaker, didn't have spiritual intelligence because when he had to anoint a king a second time, he faced yet another dilemma – appearances. We see this in the verses below:

3Then invite Jesse to the sacrifice, and I will show you what you shall do; you shall anoint for Me the one I name to you."

4So Samuel did what the Lord said, and went to Bethlehem. And the elders of the town trembled at his coming, and said, "Do you come peaceably?"

5And he said, "Peaceably; I have come to sacrifice to the Lord. Sanctify yourselves, and come with me to the sacrifice." Then he consecrated Jesse and his sons and invited them to the sacrifice.

6So it was, when they came, that he looked at Eliab and said, "Surely the Lord's anointed is before Him!" 7But, the Lord said to Samuel, "Do not look at his appearance or at his physical stature, because I have refused him. For the Lord does not see as man sees; for man looks at the outward appearance, but the Lord looks at the heart."

8 So Jesse called Abinadab, and made him pass before Samuel. And he said, "Neither has the Lord chosen this one." 9 Then Jesse made Shammah pass by. And he said, "Neither has the Lord chosen this one." 10 Thus Jesse made seven of his sons pass before Samuel. And Samuel said to Jesse, "The Lord has not chosen these." 11 And Samuel said to Jesse, "Are all the young men here?" Then he said, "There remains yet the youngest, and there he is, keeping the sheep."

And Samuel said to Jesse, "Send and bring him. For we will not sit down till he comes here." So he sent and brought him in. Now he was ruddy, with bright eyes, and good-looking. And the Lord said, "Arise, anoint him; for this is the one!"

- 1 Samuel 16:3-12 (NKJV)

From the verses above, we see that Samuel got to Jesse's house and saw Eliab: Definitely, this was king material — tall, massive, handsome – just as the first king, Saul was. He had the external qualifications and fit, and so he says to God, "My job has been made easy. The anointed of the Lord is already before me."

God burst his bubble. *"Samuel, you are old enough not to make such common mistakes. You are looking at his outward appearance. Appearances can be very deceptive."* Yes, we all know that.

I read the story of a man who was looking for a wife with only one criterion, which he believed was not a difficult request; his one desire? – A woman that does not talk much. His request proved herculean; everywhere he searched, he kept meeting talkative women. One day, he met this woman that doesn't talk at all – finally! So, as expected, he proposed to her, and she agreed to marry him. And they started planning the wedding. Then, the woman started talking. And she talked and talked, "We are going to do this and that..." The man wouldn't talk again. So everybody asked him, "Why are you not talking again?" He said, "I've already talked too much."

Appearances can be very deceptive. Some people you know to be quite noisy, other people would consider very quiet, but you'll say, "Really, then it means you don't know them." Because maybe every time you see them, they just mutter, "Good morning." They barely raise their voices until the day you see them ranting. But God Almighty is not carried away by all of that. He can say to you, "*You see this person you think is quiet; he talks too much.*" And you say, "Really?" And He says, "*Yes, o! He talks a lot.*" The Scriptures tell us that the Messiah will not judge by what He sees; He will not judge by what He hears, because all of that can be unreliable. He will judge by spiritual intelligence because an all-knowing God will give Him the information He needs. The converse is also true. We might see people who look like trouble makers, and the Spirit of God would say they are not, and you may have doubts, only for you to discover that it is true.

Designed to Save Us from Ourselves

Our shortcomings can weaken our choices on the day of vital decisions. It was King Saul's weakness for the approval of men that caused him to make faulty decisions, which ultimately ended his life and his dynasty. You can read the account in 1 Samuel 15. Spiritual intelligence saves us from the ravages of our weaknesses by giving us ample warning when we are under the pressure of diverse temptations. Sometimes, it vividly portrays the consequences of our actions to stop us from going further.

A Christian gentleman confided that he was chatting merrily with one of his ex-girlfriends on one occasion. As far as he was concerned, catching up and finding out how each of them had fared and are faring was a mere catching up. Their relationship was never physical when it existed, so emotional ties were weak and had remained so. They were just good old fashioned friends. Therefore, as far as he was concerned, it was all clean and neat, and everything was above board. Again, it was all over the telephone, and they were hoping to meet someday but had never met.

One day, he was rudely awakened from his sleep when he dreamt that his wife was determined to end their marriage. He tried to reason with her, but she was adamant. He felt it was strange and tried to persuade her to be objective and articulate her grouse, but she would not. That was when he woke up, turned around, looked at his wife, and wondered what the matter was with her that was looming in their horizon. The Holy Spirit whispered to him and warned him that if he continued to chat with his ex, sooner than later, his marriage would be at risk. He never called her after that.

Failure to Seek Intelligence

Failure, in this case, is the omission of expected action. This means that there is an existing expectation, but the person who fails does not live up to expectation. Man needs to seek God's counsel that he may benefit from His wisdom. Sometimes, God beckons to man to 'ask Him' and shows us the consequences of not doing so.

[11]*Thus saith the LORD, the Holy One of Israel, and his Maker, Ask Me of things to come concerning My sons, and concerning the work of My hands command ye Me.*

- Isaiah 45:11 (KJV)

² Ye lust, and have not: ye kill, and desire to have, and cannot obtain: ye fight and war, yet ye have not, because ye ask not.

³ Ye ask, and receive not, because ye ask amiss, that ye may consume it upon your lusts.

- James 4:2-3 (KJV)

You have not, because you ask not. Many of our problems can be traced to this prideful human instinct of jumping into things without seeking God's counsel. Failed marriages, fraud victims, accidents, failed ministries, unfulfilling careers, financial lack, physical stress, and more could have been averted by waiting on God to hear His final word.

This Scriptural statement indicted Joshua and the elders of Israel:

¹⁴Then the men of Israel took some of their provisions; but they did not ask counsel of the LORD. ¹⁵So Joshua made peace with them, and made a covenant with them to let them live, and the rulers of the congregation swore to them.

- Joshua 9:14-15 (NKJV)

In this story, Joshua and the elders of Israel signed a treaty with the Gibeonites, because they appeared with a very clever deception. They were taken in by their appearance as many are today, entering into business partnership agreements, marriage covenants, and all sorts of dealings with masters of deception. Quite a few things look so believable and evident that we become convinced that whatever the persons are saying cannot but be real. By the time you find out the actual state of affairs, it may be too late. Thank God that in this instance, the consequences were relatively harmless as revealed in Joshua 9:16-19 (NKJV):

16And it happened at the end of three days after they had made a covenant with them, that they heard that they were their neighbors who dwelt near them.

17Then the children of Israel journeyed and came to their cities on the third day. Now their cities were Gibeon, Chephirah, Beeroth, and KirjathJearim.

18But the children of Israel did not attack them, because the rulers of the congregation had sworn to them by the LORD God of Israel. And all the congregation complained against the rulers. 19Then all the rulers said to all the congregation, "We have sworn to them by the LORD God of Israel; therefore, we may not touch them.

Oaths made in the Lord's name are powerful and cannot be revoked because the Almighty God respects covenants made in His name. When Saul, in his ungodly zeal, attacked and persecuted the Gibeonites, the power of an oath sworn in the LORD's name became obvious.

1Now there was a famine in the days of David for three years, year after year; and David inquired of the LORD. The LORD said, "There is bloodguilt on Saul and on his house, because he put the Gibeonites to death."
2So the king called the Gibeonites and spoke to them. (Now the Gibeonites were not of the people of Israel, but of the remnant of the Amorites; although the people of Israel had sworn to spare them, Saul had tried to wipe them out in his zeal for the people of Israel and Judah.)

3David said to the Gibeonites, "What shall I do for you? How shall I make expiation, that you may bless the heritage of the LORD?" 4The Gibeonites said to him, "It is not a matter of silver or gold between us and Saul or his house; neither is it for us to put anyone to death in Israel." He said, "What do you say that I should do for you?"

5They said to the king, "The man who consumed us and planned to destroy us so that we should have no place in all the territory of Israel —

6let seven of his sons be handed over to us, and we will impale them before the LORD at Gibeon on the mountain of the LORD." The king said, "I will hand them over."

- 2 Samuel 21:1-6 (KJV)

When we fail to seek spiritual intelligence, we may commit disastrous errors that come to haunt us, days, or even years later, as in this case.

A Fleeing David's Failure to Seek Spiritual Intelligence

We often come across stories that reveal to us that failure to seek spiritual intelligence can have severe consequences. This can happen when we are under great pressure like David was in 1 Samuel 27:1-4.

1David said in his heart, "I shall now perish one day by the hand of Saul; there is nothing better for me than to escape to the land of the Philistines; then Saul will despair of seeking me any longer within the borders of Israel, and I shall escape out of his hand." 2So David set out and went over, he and the six hundred men who were with him, to King Achish son of Maoch of Gath.

3David stayed with Achish at Gath, he and his troops, every man with his household, and David with his two wives, Ahinoam of Jezreel, and Abigail of Carmel, Nabal's widow. 4When Saul was told that David had fled to Gath, he no longer sought for him.

- 1 Samuel 27:1-4 (NRSV)

Pressure can make a person react in haste rather than respond in wisdom. Suddenly, extending a hand of fellowship to the Philistines, Saul's arch enemies, became an excellent idea to David. The move he made was logical and made a whole lot of sense strategically. It was quite successful in the short term. Saul gave up chasing him. It would appear that the human strategy – 'the enemy of my enemy is my friend' had paid off.

The Future King of Israel Saved From Shedding Israeli Blood in War

The war between Israel and the Philistines was practically endless because they were neighbors. Soon there was another one, and King Achish decided that David should come with him to battle.

1In those days, the Philistines gathered their forces for war, to fight against Israel. Achish said to David, "You know, of course, that you and your men are to go out with me in the army." 2David said to Achish, "Very well, then you shall know what your servant can do." Achish said to David, "Very well, I will make you my bodyguard for life."

- 1 Samuel 28:1-2 (NRSV)

The LORD used the lords of the Philistines to save his neck as it were.

6Then Achish called David and said to him, "As the LORD lives, you have been honest, and to me, it seems right that you should march out and in with me in the campaign; for I have found nothing wrong in you from the day of your coming to me until today. Nevertheless, the lords do not approve of you. 7So go back now, and go peaceably; do nothing to displease the lords of the Philistines."

- 1 Samuel 29:6-7 (NRSV)

Disaster at Ziklag

After being rejected by the lords of the Philistines, David and his men made their way back to Ziklag, the city given to them by Achish. The disaster that could occur when we fail to seek spiritual intelligence stared them in the face on arrival.

¹Now when David and his men came to Ziklag on the third day, the Amalekites had made a raid on the Negeb and on Ziklag. They had attacked Ziklag, burned it down, ²and taken captive the women and all who were in it, both small and great; they killed none of them, but carried them off, and went their way.

³When David and his men came to the city, they found it burned down, and their wives and sons and daughters taken captive.

- 1 Samuel 30:1-3 (NRSV)

It was a logical decision to go and hide from Saul in the land of the Philistines. It worked but created loyalty problems that the lords of the

Philistines helped avoid. But what it meant was that while David and his men were away in Achish's service, their home in Ziklag was left wholly unprotected. The disaster almost led to a rebellion by his hitherto band of loyal troops.

⁵David's two wives also had been taken captive, Ahinoam of Jezreel, and Abigail the widow of Nabal of Carmel. ⁶David was in great danger; for the people spoke of stoning him, because all the people were bitter in spirit for their sons and daughters. But David strengthened himself in the LORD his God.

- 1 Samuel 30:5-6 (NRSV)

There are rational decisions that seem perfect when viewed from the point of human intelligence, but they open up your defenses in areas that are close to your heart. A wrong business decision can weaken a marriage. You don't see it at first, but circumstances that lead to that one wrong business decision as the foundational problem may unfold in the future. Intellect cannot consider everything; only spiritual intelligence is accurate with the past, present, and future; therefore, it provides reliable information for you to act on. If David had sought God's opinion before going to Achish, the Lord would have shown him where to hide so that Saul could never find him. In later years, God did that for Elijah when King Ahab was looking for him as revealed in 1 Kings 18:7-11 (NRSV):

7As Obadiah was on the way, Elijah met him; Obadiah recognized him, fell on his face, and said, "Is it you, my lord Elijah?" 8He answered him, "It is I. Go, tell your lord that Elijah is here." 9And he said, "How have I sinned, that you would hand your servant over to Ahab, to kill me?

10As the LORD your God lives, there is no nation or kingdom to which my lord has not sent to seek you; and when they would say, 'He is not here,' he would require an oath of the kingdom or nation, that they had not found you. 11But now you say, 'Go, tell your lord that Elijah is here.'

But David repented from his logical ways and sought spiritual intelligence before embarking on his next move to recover his family and treasures.

⁷David said to the priest, Abiathar son of Ahimelech, "Bring me the ephod." So Abiathar brought the ephod to David. ⁸David inquired of the LORD, "Shall I pursue this band? Shall I overtake them?" He answered him, "Pursue, for you shall surely overtake and shall surely rescue."

- 1 Samuel 30:7-8 (NRSV)

But someone could ask, "But what else was there to do but to pursue the people?" David had learned from experience that no matter how obvious your next move may look, you are always safer seeking spiritual intelligence. This is because our God alone knows how we should go so that we may succeed in all our endeavors. A guaranteed outcome is of the Lord, as the end of this story revealed in 1 Samuel 30:18-19 (NRSV):

¹⁸David recovered all that the Amalekites had taken, and David rescued his two wives.
¹⁹Nothing was missing, whether small or great, sons or daughters, spoil or anything that had been taken; David brought back everything.

CHAPTER 3

Spiritual Intelligence and
Business Decisions

How can one know the outcome of a business venture? A lady learned that there was much profit in commodity trade. She immediately borrowed money and plunged in. It looked so easy. Source the commodity, truck it to the depot, have the supervisor certify it, and bingo, outcomes your cheque at the other end. Sourcing the product was not a problem at all. The bottleneck was finding the supervisor to certify its quality. The trucks that delivered her stock to the warehouse waited endlessly for this supervisor, but he was nowhere to be found.

Unknown to her, supervisors only appear by appointment and by special arrangement. As she ran around, searching for this invisible supervisor, the demurrage on the delivery trucks started mounting, and the commodity was beginning to rot. She pulled every conceivable string she knew to pull, but no supervisor appeared on her horizon. Finally, by the time he appeared, he downgraded her product's quality due to poor storage, and she had to find her own money to pay back the bank loan in full.

Spiritual intelligence would simply have warned her that what you see is not really what you get as there is a lot more to this commodity business than meets the eye. When profit alone drives our zeal, we may enter into diverse snares that cause us great anguish.

Right Analysis, Wrong Decision

You and I can easily be fooled. That is why it is important to study how our Lord Jesus operated because He is our example in everything. Our Lord always had information. If you and I were in His position and had to choose the twelve apostles to carry the redemption message to all humanity, we wouldn't have chosen those people—fishermen, illiterates? No! We would have looked out for rabbis and educated men and women. Yes, we would have based our choices on qualifications, experience, and high sounding dissertations. But what did our Lord Jesus do? He chose fishers!

Somebody said there must be something about fishermen because of all the twelve apostles, about five or six were fishermen. I did a little study on that, and one of the things I discovered is that fishermen are used to working together. They like to work together. They don't work alone. When they had that miracle of a lot of fishes, they just beckoned to their other colleagues, and immediately, they came to help. Maybe there is something about that, but the amazing thing is that our Lord Jesus chose ordinary people, and they did the work. Anybody could have told Him, "No, You are going to the wrong people." But because our Lord had intelligence, He put together a team that God could use.

Another story in the Bible supporting this concept of right analysis, wrong decisions, is Eli's story, the priest, Samuel's mentor. Eli didn't measure up to the responsibility of being a priest and a judge. In his days, the priest was also the judge. His children were corrupt, but he did not call them to order. When this was going on in Israel, a certain woman without a child, Hannah, went to bargain with God in prayer as it were and said: "*Lord, You need a prophet and I need a son. Okay, we can meet each other halfway.*" And so Hannah got a son, and God got a prophet. Decades down the line, we find her son, Samuel, now old, sitting as judge and prophet over Israel and his children turning out like Eli's children. The interesting thing about spiritual intelligence is that you can make the right analysis but still make the wrong decision. The children of Israel came to Samuel and said: "Your children are not following in your ways; make us a king to enable us to be like other nations." You see, that was the wrong conclusion. The analysis was right; immoral and irresponsible people cannot be the judge because they are not examples to lead or inspire, but then what is the solution? Only God can say what the solution is. They got a stopgap king—Saul, for forty years before their king was ready—David.

We mustn't make decisions based on the fact that we have looked at the matter carefully, analyzed it thoroughly, and worked it out. All of that is good, but we must let God guide the decision at the end of the day. Nobody is decrying, looking at the issues, analyzing them, and thinking them over, but we must choose to let God guide the decision at the end of the day. The value of intelligence is prevention.

Some time ago, a friend came and introduced a business idea to me. It was trading in groundnuts. He said that the business was very lucrative in Russia and would yield a three hundred percent profit margin. I told him to let me pray about it before I gave my response. During what was a praying session for decision making, God said to me, *"Do not turn to a groundnut seller because of money."* That closed the chapter for me. I told my friend that I would not venture into the business. Six months later, I asked him about the outcome of the venture: he said that he could sell only one container out of three and that the remaining two had become infested with bugs. That is why you and I need spiritual intelligence to reduce heartaches from errors. How often do you involve God in your decision-making process? Do you run ahead of Him only to end up in a bind, screaming for deliverance?

God is an economist, He is an engineer, and He is a doctor. He can help you, and I make complicated decisions. There is no profession, no calling where God is not informed. He is the author of all things, and when we ask Him for wisdom, counsel, and guidance, few years down the road, we are amazed at the wonders of the decisions that we have taken today because we received them from God. God helps us and also stops us from making a fool of ourselves many times. That's very important. You know sometimes by the time God stops you from making a decision, a few months or years down the road, you'll put your two hands on your head and scream in relief and wonder because you would have made a complete fool of yourself if you had continued on the road you were going. No Christian should function without intelligence. Our Lord and Saviour, Jesus Christ, came to save the world, but He did it with spiritual intelligence.

You see, He said to us that He came to the earth to accomplish the will of the Father who sent Him and not His own. One of the things that can fascinate you is to study the man—Jesus, not God but the man. By the time you look at the man, how He handled His situations, you will be amazed. I can never forget some of those Scriptures like when the Jews came to say to Him, "Master, we know that you're fearless, you don't regard personalities, and speak the word of

God in truth." If it were you and I, we would have been carried away, but our Lord Jesus by His response, seemed to say, "So what's the catch? What exactly do you want?" Like your child comes to you and says, "Daddy, you're wonderful," and rather than give an excited reply, you say, "No no, no! Just tell me what you want."

Now, the Jewish leaders turned around and said, "Tell us, is it right to pay taxes to Caesar?" It was a catch question because if He had said, '*Pay taxes to Caesar*,' they would have said that He was unpatriotic. If He had said, '*Don't pay taxes to Caesar*,' they would have run to Pilate. Throwing them off guard, our Lord said, "Show Me your coin."

This they did. Then He asked, "Whose inscription is this?"
"Caesar's," they said.

"Render to Caesar what belongs to Caesar and God what belongs to God," He concluded. They were speechless.

22"*When they had heard these words, they marveled, and left Him and went their way.*"

- Matthew 22:22 (NKJV)

You see, that is the wonder when we follow the path that our Lord Jesus had trod so that God's purposes can come through.

Spiritual intelligence is vital in the business world because there are all sorts of dangers as you navigate the waters of business life. It works to protect you. In Jacob and Laban's story, Jacob had served a hard master who was also his father-in-law, and he decided to run away from him, taking away his acquired possessions, his wives, and children. Laban was cross with Jacob on several counts – First, because he believed that Jacob had enriched himself from his business and wealth; he also thought Jacob's wives (his daughters) and children (his grandchildren) belonged to him. Laban was determined to take those children back and hurt Jacob, but God stepped into the situation:

[29]*"It is in my power to do you harm, but the God of your father spoke to me last night, saying, 'Be careful that you speak to Jacob neither good nor bad.'*

- Genesis 31:29 (NKJV)

Laban confessed that he would have dealt with him if not that God had forewarned him. God knew the thoughts and intents of Laban's heart. But for God, it would not have gone well with Jacob. In our offices and networks, we operate in the marketplace, not knowing the thoughts and intents of the persons who interact with us. Facial expressions do not always reveal true intentions. That's what I tell people who are managers and CEOs - I say, "Listen. When you come to a meeting and people are talking, you don't know where they are coming from and their secret agenda. Therefore, there is a simple prayer that you should pray as a person in management:

"Lord, while these men and women are talking, please listen to them."

Yes – God is the one that needs to listen to them because when they finish speaking, He will then tell you whether any of the people is speaking for Him because God can speak through anybody. You need that intelligence to filter everything people are saying or doing so that when you make decisions, they will be conclusions that heaven will backup and that God's power will come down on.

Somebody said that when you get to heaven and the Lord unveils your life and you see all the dangers and pitfalls you narrowly escaped, you will kneel again and thank the Lord! Because we don't know everything, a little obedience has achieved like, *'Stay here for two minutes.'* If that man had stayed in that petrol station for five minutes, he would never have discovered what he missed until maybe he gets to heaven, and the scene is recalled to him. People who are not accustomed to obeying God's voice miss out a lot on the benefits of receiving information details that avert the enemy's plans. As a result, they run into all kinds of errors and dangers. The reason is that sometimes, God will warn you – send people, do many things to catch your attention, or inspire your obedience. But at other times, He may only say it once, and He won't mention it again.

And you and I need to be conversant with all this. I say to people that part of the things we learn in the journey of life is that God has signboards and warnings as we journey through life, and that's why you should slow down on your speed quite often, so you don't miss some signposts. Some of them are on billboards, so it doesn't matter how fast you're going; you can still read them. But some of them are posters. That means you have to slow down. Some of them are handbills, and that means that you have to stop to read them. Now some of them are handwritten; you not only have to stop, but you also have to bend over. Then some of them are written in faded ink. You have to study them to decipher them.

Those who are familiar with God and His ways recognize these different communication modalities and, with time, develop the sensitivities needed to respond to each message type correctly. And it's essential to understand this because God wants every Christian to be strong and effective by using all the resources He has made available. To live a Christian life without intelligence is like climbing a mountain without ropes—you're going to be crashing ever so often. And many people are crashing ever so often because they miss out on intelligence, those precious divine signals, and are busy rushing along. God wants you and me to pause and wait on Him to hear what He has to say about every issue confronting us. That is why the Bible says we walk by faith and not by sight. Everything may look good, and the Spirit could still say no!

When I was trying to set up my business, I couldn't get a bank loan. I tried several times without success. Then, a friend of mine invited me to come and join their practice. I went there and discussed terms with them, and they were ready to take me on. They said to me, "Whenever you get your kidney machine, just bring it here. We'll work together." And there are many reasons we should have worked together because one of the partners is a surgeon, and I'm a physician. But when I came back from that meeting, God whispered to me, "*This place you are headed, is not the thing I want for you.*"

I waited a month, two months, and when I didn't get any loan, I called them up again, and we had a second discussion. When I got home, God said to me again, "I've *told you that that place you are going is not the place.*" Waiting often wearies our patience. So I waited another month, two months, three months, nothing happened. I called them up yet again. However, the night before we had that third meeting, I had a dream where I was harvesting yams and putting them in a heap behind me, and a man and a woman came with baskets and were carrying the yams away. Some dreams don't need any interpretation. And amazingly, two weeks after, the bank gave me a loan, so I almost blew it!

That's why I say to you that you and I need spiritual intelligence. The story of my life could have been different from then on. God wants you and me to stay on that road that will ensure that we become and do everything in His heart for us.

CHAPTER 4

How to Be Wired to Receive
Spiritual Intelligence

Radios and telephones are wired to transmit and receive radio signals. And for this to happen, they have to be within the range of the base station. People who walk in the spirit are within the base station range and will receive the intelligence transmitted from the spirit realm.

1After these things, Jesus walked in Galilee:

for he would not walk in Jewry, because the Jews sought to kill him.2 Now the Jew's feast of tabernacles was at hand.

3His brethren therefore said unto him, Depart hence, and go into Judaea, that thy disciples also may see the works that thou doest. ⁴For there is no man that doeth anything in secret, and he himself seeketh to be known openly. If thou do these things, shew thyself to the world.

⁵For neither did his brethren believe in him. ⁶Then Jesus said unto them, My time is not yet come: but your time is always ready. ⁷The world cannot hate you; but me it hateth, because I testify of it, that the works thereof are evil. ⁸Go ye up unto this feast: I go not up yet unto this feast: for my time is not yet full come."

- John 7:1-8 (KJV)

Our Lord Jesus demonstrated or modeled how we should live our lives here on earth. He was telling His brethren that they could go to Jerusalem anytime they liked, but He could not do that because He was under threat for His life. He knew that His life and His death must be according to God's plan.

Be Led By the Spirit

Spiritual people don't do things simply because others are doing it; they must get approval from heaven, ensuring that everything is alright. That is why many Christians run into all sorts of troubles because they do not get intelligence.

6"Now the mind of the flesh is death [both now and forever — because it pursues sin]; but the mind of the Spirit is life and peace [the spiritual well-being that comes from walking with God — both now and forever];"

– Romans 8:6 (AMP)

Our Lord Jesus told His brothers that He was not concerned with what people were doing or saying. He did not need the approval of men. As a Christian, all you need is heaven's approval. Let the whole world say 'no,' but if God says 'yes' –then 'yes' it must be, and that's all you need.

The people, particularly their leaders, expected our Lord Jesus to show up at the beginning of the feast, but He did not get there until the middle of the feast. He came in quietly and went to the temple to teach the people. When the Pharisees heard that He was there, they sent soldiers to arrest Him, but they could not touch Him because He was walking with God's timing and so under the protection of God's invisible army. I want you to know that you and I need spiritual intelligence.

In the Old Testament, it was a preserve of prophets. Today, however, it is for everybody 'wired' to God by His Holy Spirit, because the Bible says, "In the last days I will pour my Spirit upon all flesh." That means that intelligence is available to every Christian. In the olden days, people used to go and consult seers when they had problems. This kind of consultation happened in the case of Saul. When he was looking for his father's asses, he went to meet Samuel.

Likewise, the verses below show the prophet, Elisha operating with spiritual intelligence:

8Then the king of Syria warred against Israel, and took counsel with his servants, saying, In such and such a place shall be my camp. 9And the man of God sent unto the king of Israel, saying, Beware that thou pass not such a place; for thither the Syrians are come down. 10And the king of Israel sent to the place which the man of God told him and warned him of, and saved himself there, not once nor twice.

11Therefore the heart of the king of Syria was sore troubled for this thing; and he called his servants, and said unto them, Will ye not shew me which of us is for the king of Israel? 12And one of his servants said, None, my lord, O king: but Elisha, the prophet that is in Israel, telleth the king of Israel the words that thou speakest in thy bedchamber. –

- 2 Kings 6:8-12 (NKJV)

The King of Syria thought that someone from his camp revealed his secrets spoken in his bedroom to the King of Israel. He was not aware that there was a man of God in Israel who had access to his plans by revelation until one of his soldiers told him about Elisha. So, prophets were men who knew about events to come, by the Spirit of God. They walked in revelation knowledge, and God spoke in their ears and caused them to see into the spirit realm. It was open knowledge that men came to inquire from them concerning their issues and to know what the Lord is saying.

Sadly, in this dispensation, when God has equalized this virtue by grace, many would still rather consult with prophets, men of God, and all sorts of third parties to hear God on their behalf than seek God for themselves. They say such things like, "Man of God, what is the Lord saying?" That is why so many have become victims of deception and are at the mercy of charlatans and sorcerers.

A woman came to meet me in Church some time ago and said to me, "I heard that your Church denomination is very powerful, but I need to ask if you see?"

I said to her, "We have eyes, and we do see."

She sounded a little exasperated at my response. It seemed to her that I had not understood her question. "Nooo!" she said, "I mean, do you see visions?"

I told her that we don't see visions for people, but we train people to see their visions.

And that is the problem that the whole world is facing. Even people in authority look for someone to have revelations and hear from God on their behalf. In this search for revelation knowledge, some resort to astrology, seances, and the occult for help. Access to revelation insight is what the Lord gave to His Church freely by the Holy Spirit. You need to desire it if you don't have it. You have to get because it is indispensable to spiritual life. You can't walk on the wisdom of men alone. No, you can't. Once you can get your spiritual intelligence by yourself, then you have become the prophet you need. Nobody can manipulate you. Have you seen how some of these charlatan prophets manipulate and deceive people?

There was one woman who went for prayers and paid N800 there for consultation. It would appear that when the man needed more money, he sent for her to come for new prayers, for according to him, there was a looming threat of death over her life. His message to her was, "*Ikunbo! Ikunbo!*" which means, "Death is coming," but if you can get your revelation by yourself, nobody needs to frighten you with such a message. If a real threat or danger is looming, the Holy Spirit will reveal it to you.

In the New Testament, Apostle Paul operates this way; although persecuted and in chains for the Gospel, he remained in charge of His environment by speaking God's mind. Spiritual intelligence ensures that you retain your authority irrespective of the storms and perils of life.

"And he said unto them, Sirs, I perceive that this voyage will be with hurt and much damage, not only of the lading and ship but also of our lives. Nevertheless, the centurion believed the master and the owner of the ship, more than those things which were spoken by Paul. And because the haven was not commodious to winter in, the more part advised to depart thence also, if by any means they might attain to Phenice, and there to winter; which is a haven of Crete, and lieth toward the southwest and northwest. And when the south wind blew softly, supposing that they had obtained their purpose, loosing thence, they sailed close by Crete. But not long after, there arose against it a tempestuous wind, called Euroclydon. And when the

ship was caught, and could not bear up into the wind, we let her drive."

- Acts 27:10-15 (KJV)

Paul informed the people with him on the ship about the intelligence he had received from the above passage, but they did not believe him because everything was calm and stable, and besides, he was not a sailor. The most dangerous thing in life is for the devil to plot to deceive you. After receiving an intelligence report to avert a mishap, you ignore it because the present situation does not indicate that what the Holy Spirit is saying is on your horizon. The centurion and the shipmaster neglected Paul's warnings, but not quite long after, disaster struck.

You may have experienced situations where you wanted to go somewhere, but God did not allow you to go; and the following day, you went out, only to discover why God told you not to go. God has reasons for His instructions.

Seek God's Approval Before You Venture

We can learn a lot from the life of David. David was a man who typically would never venture unless God approved the next move or strategy. His approach can be seen in 2 Samuel 5:17-25 (KJV):

[17]Now when the Philistines heard that they had anointed David king over Israel, all the Philistines went up to search for David. And David heard of it and went down to the stronghold. [18]The Philistines also went and deployed themselves in the Valley of Rephaim. [19]So David inquired of the Lord, saying, "Shall I go up against the Philistines? Will You deliver them into my hand?"

And the Lord said to David, "Go up, for I will doubtless deliver the Philistines into your hand."

[20]So David went to Baal Perazim, and David defeated them there; and he said, "The Lord has broken through my enemies before me, like a breakthrough of water."

Therefore he called the name of that place Baal Perazim. 21And they left their images there, and David and his men carried them away.

22Then the Philistines went up once again and deployed themselves in the Valley of Rephaim. 23Therefore David inquired of the Lord, and He said, "You shall not go up; circle around behind them, and come upon them in front of the mulberry trees. 24And it shall be, when you hear the sound of marching in the tops of the mulberry trees, then you shall advance quickly. For then the Lord will go out before you to strike the camp of the Philistines." 25And David did so, as the Lord commanded him; and he drove back the Philistines from Geba as far as Gezer.

David never relied on past successes to confront present challenges. He always sought the face of the Lord for each occasion. Today, sadly, there are many Christians that rely on their experiences. Once God answers them in a particular way, they make that the pattern and formula when other problems come up. Generally, we know that quite a few people like to use formulas because they make life easier. But you and I know that if formulas determined true success in life, men wouldn't need God anymore.

From the text in 2 Kings 6, talking about Elisha, Elisha was distinguished because when his master, Elijah, was about to leave the earth, he asked Elisha what he wanted him to do for him. Elisha asked for a double portion of Elijah's anointing. The anointing made him do outstanding miracles, and that was why he could have insights into the plans of the King of Syria and relay them to the King of Israel.

Elisha was an Old Testament prophet, and we have a better covenant as believers in Christ Jesus. If an Old Testament prophet could be so spiritually intelligent, then we of the Grace dispensation have no excuse. Elisha's story has more to teach:

"And he said, Go and spy where he is, that I may send and fetch him. And it was told him, saying, Behold, he is in Dothan. Therefore sent he thither horses, and chariots, and a great host: and they came by night and compassed the city about.

And when the servant of the man of God was risen early, and gone forth, behold, an host compassed the city both with horses and chariots. And his servant said unto him, Alas, my master! How shall we do?

And he answered, Fear not: for they that be with us are more than they that be with them. And Elisha prayed, and said, Lord, I pray thee, open his eyes, that he may see.

And the Lord opened the eyes of the young man; and he saw: and, behold, the mountain was full of horses and chariots of fire round about Elisha. And when they came down to him, Elisha prayed unto the Lord, and said, Smite this people, I pray thee, with blindness. And he smote them with blindness according to the word of Elisha. And

Elisha said unto them, This is not the way, neither is this the city: follow me, and I will bring you to the man whom ye seek. But he led them to Samaria."

- 2 Kings 6:13-18 (KJV)

Gehazi was ruled by fear until Elisha prayed that God should open his eyes to see the heavenly host with them. Are you often afraid when faced with daunting circumstances? Perhaps you need spiritual intelligence to bolster your courage and faith when problems confront you. It is available to you for the asking.

Connect Your Spirit with the Spirit of God

You don't need your mind alone to make your decisions. You must rely on God for that because everything lies open before Him. I want you to know that mind based decisions depend on the information available from past events, present happenings, and future projections, which are still limited. Nobody can be sure of the facts in their entirety, and the truth of the matter is, you can only know the past and present in part, but it is only God that knows the future. And if this is so, how then can I access such information from Him?

"But God hath revealed them unto us by his Spirit: for the Spirit searcheth all things, yea, the deep things of God. For what man knoweth the things of a man, save the spirit of man which is in him? even so, the things of God knoweth no man, but the Spirit of God. Now we have received, not the spirit of the world, but the spirit which is of God; that we might know the things that are freely given to us of God."

- 1 Corinthians 2:10-12 (KJV)

And the Bible says in John 4:24 that "*God is a Spirit: and they that worship Him must worship Him in spirit and truth.*" We should know that spirit does not communicate with flesh, and your mind is flesh, so you need to get to the realm of the spirit to receive from God. The spirit in man gives us physical life. But for it to provide us with spiritual insight, it has to be hooked up with the Spirit of God for only the Spirit of God has access to all that the Creator of the universe knows and sees. Our Lord Jesus Christ made this point to Nicodemus when He said to him, *"You must be born again."* This new birth, our Lord Jesus further explained, comes through the Word and the Spirit of God. He distinguished the natural birth from the spiritual birth when He said in John 3:6 (NKJV):

"That which is born of the flesh is flesh, and that which is born of the Spirit is spirit."

The Bible tells us that to be born of the Spirit is to be born of God. The process is explained in John 1:12-13 (NKJV)

"But as many as received Him, to them He gave the right to become children of God, to those who believe in

His name: who were born, not of blood, nor of the will of the flesh, nor of the will of man, but of God."

When a man receives Jesus Christ in his heart as his personal Lord and Saviour, his sins are forgiven him by God Almighty. This is because our Lord Jesus paid the penalty for sins for all humanity when He shed His blood and died on the Cross of Calvary. That was the sacrifice that provided the pardon so that our Father in heaven can freely forgive men their sins without violating His justice. And to receive that pardon and be rewired or hooked up with the Spirit of God, the man must confess that Jesus Christ is his Lord and Saviour so he can benefit from the pardon He obtained for all humanity on the Cross of Calvary. It is a straightforward birth process detailed in Romans 10:8-10 (NLT2):

[8]The message is very close at hand; it is on your lips and in your heart." And that message is the very message about faith that we preach:

9If you confess with your mouth that Jesus is Lord and believe in your heart that God raised him from the dead, you will be saved.

10For it is by believing in your heart that you are made right with God, and it is by confessing with your mouth that you are saved."

Following on the new birth, our capacity to receive spiritual intelligence receives a great boost through the Holy Spirit's baptism. When we are baptized in the Holy Spirit, we can speak in other tongues, which serves to nourish our spiritual life by building us up in our most holy faith (Jude 1:20). Holy Spirit baptism is further to sensitize your spirit and quicken the link to the Spirit of God. He will energize your human spirit with added capacity to receive messages from God.

To get intelligence from God then, you must be ready to surrender your will to His will. Your prayers then become, 'Lord, let Your will be done in everything and every area of my life.' When we understand that God has unlimited knowledge about anything and everything, we grow in confidence in submitting our will and desires to His control, with a commitment to do as He says in every area of life. Even if you are in dire need of something and ask Him in prayer, and He says no, then 'no' it must be. If you are committed to this, the communication channel to spiritual intelligence will be empowered. It is unqualified obedience to the will of God that fully unlocks the gates to spiritual intelligence. And the more we obey His directives, the better the channel will function for God's desire for us is that we live our lives like His Son, Jesus did here on earth.

28Then Jesus said to them, "When you lift up the Son of Man, then you will know that I am He, and that I do nothing of Myself; but as My Father taught Me, I speak these things.

29And He who sent Me is with Me. The Father has not left Me alone, for I always do those things that please Him."

- John 8:28-29 (NKJV)

Summary Of How To Be Wired For Spiritual Intelligence

- Accept the Lord Jesus Christ as your personal Lord and Saviour. This will cause the spirit within you to reconnect with the Spirit of God, and this in turn will re-establish the communication channel for spiritual intelligence in your soul.

- Seek the baptism of the Holy Spirit with the added gift of speaking in tongues. Speaking in tongues serves to bolster this spiritual connection between the spirit in man and the Spirit of God.

- Desire to be led by the Spirit of God in all things, for as the Scripture teaches, those who are led by the Spirit of God are truly children of God. Also, when the Spirit of God leads us, we progressively conform to the image of Christ, our Saviour. In our creation, the purpose of God revealed in Romans 8:29, is that we be conformed into the image of Christ.

- The line of communication is that when we desire to know God's mind on any matter, the Spirit of God will search the mind of God to extract what He has decided. Having obtained that information, He will communicate it to the spirit in you, and the spirit in you will deliver it to your mind. When the communication channel is free-flowing, facilitated by previous obedience, this channel can flow almost unhindered. Sometimes, however, we may wait a while to receive it. But no matter how long it takes, we must wait to know how we should go from the Lord.

CHAPTER 5

Empowering the Saints through Spiritual Intelligence

Empowerment means that you walk in the confidence, ability, and authority of the new birth. Our Lord Jesus spoke of 'authority' and 'power' to His disciples when He talked about the Holy Spirit, overcoming the enemy's power and effectively witnessing as God's Kingdom representatives on earth.

"I have given you authority to trample on snakes and scorpions and to overcome all the power of the enemy; nothing will harm you."

- Luke 10:19 (NIV)

"Then Jesus came to them and said, "All authority in heaven and on earth has been given to Me. Therefore, go and make disciples of all nations, baptizing them in the name of the Father, and of the Son, and of the Holy Spirit."

- Matthew 28:18-19 (BSB)

"But you will receive power when the Holy Spirit comes on you, and you will be My witnesses in Jerusalem, and in all Judea and Samaria, and to the ends of the earth."

- Acts 1:8 (NIV)

To receive the Holy Spirit is to receive power. Spiritual intelligence is a source of empowerment for the saints to live adequately and successfully on the earth. Spiritual intelligence will heighten your perception and give you discernment to see things as they are, no matter how authentic they sound. By this insight, Paul was able to tell between a spirit of divination and a true prophecy.

[16] *Now it happened, as we went to prayer, that a certain slave girl possessed with a spirit of divination met us, who brought her masters much profit by fortune-telling.* [17]*This*

girl followed Paul and us, and cried out, saying, "These men are the servants of the Most High God, who proclaim to us the way of salvation." ¹⁸And this she did for many days. But Paul, greatly annoyed, turned and said to the spirit, "I command you in the name of Jesus Christ to come out of her." And he came out that very hour.

- Acts 16: 16-18 (NKJV)

When empowered with spiritual intelligence, the saints can stand out in trying times and come through the most challenging circumstances that could have destroyed their faith. The late Kenneth E. Hagin described it some years ago. He said that two years before the bubble burst in the mid-80s, the Spirit of God had spoken that the bubble would burst, and he was advised to cut down and readjust. He said he took all the necessary precautions, and he downsized his organization and all the people he laid off got jobs before the bubble burst. He said, "When the bubble finally burst," I was there in America, "many ministries would come on television and say, "Send at least $5, or we will not be here next week'. It was a cry of desperation. But the man who had intelligence prepared for the time and the season of leanness and had no need to be desperate.

God always sends intelligence information to His people because He does not want them to fail. God does not want you to fail; that's why He warns you. And if you and I do not have intelligence, then we are at a disadvantage. When people stand up for God in difficult circumstances, they do not do it in their strength. They must have the backing of the Holy Spirit. They must have information that keeps them always up ahead, which gives them the advantage they need.

One day, in Luke 22:21, our Lord Jesus told Peter that the devil had asked for permission to sift him like wheat, and the permission was granted. To avert the destruction of your faith, I have prayed for you that when it is all over, your faith in Me and God will survive. There are conversations in the spirit realm that determine physical outcomes. We see a similar occurrence in the life of Job. He was going about his business when, unknown to him, discussions about him were ongoing in the spirit realm. In Peter's case, we are thankful that he had the intercessory ministry of our Lord Jesus Christ, who knew about the devil's request and had acted on that intelligence and prayed for Peter.

When our Lord Jesus left the earth, it seems His disciples were done for, but He understood that the Christian is vulnerable without the help and intelligence that the Holy Spirit provides, so He made a promise – "I will not leave you as orphans, I will come to you."

"And I will pray the Father, and He will give you another Helper, that He may abide with you forever – the Spirit of truth, whom the world cannot receive, because it neither

sees Him nor knows Him; but you know Him, for He dwells with you and will be in you. I will not leave you orphans; I will come to you."

- John 14:16-18 (NKJV)

An orphan is a child whose parents are dead. In essence, the Holy Spirit is the God-head's parenting presence, fathering, directing, and protecting the believer on earth. A father is one who gives a child protective care, a provider, and an instructor. When He was about leaving the earth, our Lord Jesus promised the coming of the Holy Spirit. So, even though the Lord is no longer physically present on earth, the Holy Spirit has been given to us to provide us with the same spiritual intelligence that He had. Fortunately, this is available to every believer.

"But when He, the Spirit of Truth, comes, He will guide you into all the truth [full and complete truth]. For He will not speak on His own initiative, but He will speak whatever He hears [from the Father — the message regarding the Son], and He will disclose to you what is to

come [in the future]. He will glorify and honor Me because He (the Holy Spirit) will take from what is Mine and will disclose it to you. All things that the Father has are Mine. Because of this I said that He [the Spirit] will take from what is Mine and will reveal it to you."

- John 16:13-16 (AMP)

Years ago, I had to travel to Hawaii for the international convention of my local church assembly, and before I went there, I prayed a prayer. I said, "Lord if the devil is planning anything against me, which I'm not aware of, please reveal it to me." And that night, I had a dream. A man brought about six ladies in bikinis by the beach and said they should strip before me. Then he started to laugh at me. He began to say to me, "I've caught you now."

So I responded to him and said, "In the name of Jesus!" Immediately, they vanished, and I woke up.

Interestingly, when I had said I was going to Hawaii, people were pleased. "How wonderful," they gushed, giggling their delight. Thank God for spiritual intelligence. When I came back, they asked, "Did you go to the beach?"

I retorted, "And what would I be looking for there?"

I had intelligence before I embarked on the Hawaii trip. God wants to give us the intelligence information we need to escape the many traps of the devil. Everywhere the enemy is planning for you, no matter the extent, the Holy Spirit will reveal it to you because God does not want you to fail, no! Of what use is your failure to God? God wants to see you, and I stand firm, and so when you see a man standing strong by the Spirit of God, he has a lot of intelligence, a lot of grace. Daily, the Holy Spirit is flooding him with insight and revelation of things to come and how he needs to progress or respond. When we have spiritual intelligence, we are operating at an advantage; we are privileged to see what God sees and hear what God hears to avoid traps and dangers from the enemy and so get ahead. No wonder the Scriptures tell us to *put on the whole armour of God that you may be able to withstand the devil's wiles or tricks (Ephesians 6:11)*

I shared this testimony some years ago. From nowhere, I had this revelation, and it was a Sunday morning. I was using my car to transport people to Sunday school, and then I came home. I found my daughter and her friend at home. They hadn't gone to Church, and there at home with them were these two boys with Mike Tyson's style haircut; that was in the days when it was in vogue. I said to them, "What are you guys doing here? Come on, go to Church!" So, I woke up, wondering what this was all about, but I kept my ears open. Suddenly, my wife and my daughter were arguing, "If you say that, you are not going to that party again."

I said, "Which party?"

"My friend is having a birthday party," my daughter answered. I said nobody was going to any party. My daughter was surprised, but I insisted because I heard God. To receive the Holy Spirit is to receive unusual capacity and ability. He will disclose to you what is to come in the future.

A while ago, we were in England for Christmas, and my daughter was celebrating her birthday. Her pastor came to her celebration, and in conversing with him, he said to us that when she was single before she got married, they used to talk to her about boys, and they said she told them, "Soon, my father will have a dream."

You can never really understand what God is doing—putting pillars in people's lives through intelligence. He did something for me and did something for her with that singular revelation.

It is simply amazing. To go on living without that kind of help is a significant disadvantage because you and I need to be always one step ahead of the devil so that God can receive glory through our lives.

Spiritual intelligence empowers you to be effective for ministry. Phillip, the evangelist, was located at the right place and time in his ministry by spiritual intelligence.

26Now an angel of the Lord spoke to Philip, saying, "Arise and go toward the south along the road which goes down from Jerusalem to Gaza." This is desert. 27So he arose and went. And behold, a man of Ethiopia, a eunuch of great authority under Candace the queen of the Ethiopians, who had charge of all her treasury, and had come to Jerusalem to worship, 28 was returning. And sitting in his chariot, he was reading Isaiah the prophet. 29Then the Spirit said to Philip, "Go near and overtake this chariot."

30So Philip ran to him, and heard him reading the prophet Isaiah, and said, "Do you understand what you are reading?"

³¹*And he said, "How can I unless someone guides me?"
And he asked Philip to come up and sit with him.* ³²*The
place in the Scripture which he read was this:*

"He was led as a sheep to the slaughter;

And as a lamb before its shearer is silent,

So He opened not His mouth.

³³*In His humiliation, His justice was taken away,*

And who will declare His generation?

For His life is taken from the earth."

³⁴*So the eunuch answered Philip and said, "I ask you, of
whom does the prophet say this, of himself or of some other
man?"* ³⁵*Then Philip opened his mouth, and beginning at
this Scripture, preached Jesus to him.*

- Acts 8:26-35 (NKJV)

The saints are guaranteed to live in the center of God's will when they follow His voice. Spiritual intelligence is the word of God revealed to you. It is incredible that Elijah, who tutored and mentored Elisha had so much insight and power that when he had that contest with Baal's prophets on Mount Carmel, he said to God: "*I want you to prove to these people that I have done everything according to your word, all of these things were not my imagination, I did not contrive them, I had clear instructions from You."*

"36At the time of sacrifice, the prophet Elijah stepped forward and prayed: "Lord, the God of Abraham, Isaac, and Israel, let it be known today that you are God in Israel and that I am your servant and have done all these things at your command. 37Answer me, Lord, answer me, so these people will know that you, Lord, are God and that you are turning their hearts back again."

- 1 Kings 18: 36-37 (NIV)

Now Elisha watched all of these and when Elijah said to him, "Ask what I should do for you before I leave you," he had no hesitation. He said "I need a double portion of your spirit. You were one step ahead of the devil, I want to be ten steps ahead."

Elisha's desire was granted, and as a result, his ministry's record was simply awesome. A preacher once called him "the Executive Prophet." Elisha predated our Lord Jesus Christ in being used by God to perform remarkable miracles like:

- He multiplied bread.

- He made an ax-head, made of iron to float on water. The sons of the prophets said the ax that they borrowed fell into the stream, and Elisha asked where it fell. He simply cut a piece of wood, threw it into the water, and then the iron surfaced.

- The prophet's widow reported to Elisha that her husband's creditors wanted to dispossess her and enslave her two sons. The prophet asked what she had at home by way of resource, and she said she had nothing. Then, she thought about it and said, "Oh, just a pot of oil."

"That will do," said Elisha. "Go and borrow basins, and then start pouring."

Elisha had so much anointing. He rarely went aside to pray when difficulties and challenges requiring solutions were brought to him. When Naaman, the Syrian army general, came to Elisha for healing, the prophet sent his servant, Gehazi, to tell Naaman not to bring leprosy into their home, and instructed that he should just go and bathe in the River Jordan seven times. Naaman was annoyed and said, "I thought he would come and attend to me," Elisha said, "Me? Touch leprosy? No. Go and bathe, and you will be healed."

He was so powerfully anointed that he hardly prayed publicly but for one occasion when the Shunammite woman came to him, and Elisha said, "Something has happened to her and God has hidden it from me. I did not get the intelligence. I didn't." That's how handicapped you and I can be when we don't get the intelligence. Elisha said, "I didn't get the intelligence on this," and he wasn't ready for it. So he gave Gehazi his rod and said to him, "Go and lay it on the boy, and he would wake up." Gehazi went and returned and said, "Oga, it didn't work o! The boy is still dead." Elisha went there, prayed, laid hands on the boy, warmed him, got up, and prayed again, all because he didn't have intelligence. And that's what can happen to you and me; when we don't have that vital intelligence information, we struggle. Yes! Every time we don't have intelligence, we struggle, but once we have intelligence, we are prepared; we are one step ahead, we are equipped and have gone before our God to be empowered.

Desire a New Dimension of Spiritual Life

God wants you to operate with intelligence, and every time God puts you in a place, He wants to supply you with the information you need to succeed in that place, glorify His name, and make Him known. He desires to empower and alert you before events happen. He will prepare you. He will give you instructions and directions. That's the way He has designed us to be Christians in this world. There is no other way for a Christian to bring glory to God on the earth. We are called to be like Christ in this world.

We are not here on earth to make decisions independently; we are here to receive instructions from heaven about every situation that confronts us, and to carry out God ordered instructions for our benefit and to His glory. When we let God instruct and direct us in everything we do, His name is glorified, and we are blessed in our ways. But you and I have to have the right priorities. We have to make the proper requests.

The Bible says in 1Kings 3 that after Solomon became king, God came to him in a dream and asked, "*Solomon, what do you want me to do for you?*" And Solomon replied, "You have made me king O God, and I'm a child. I need a discerning spirit so that I can judge your people correctly."

Now, this is a dream. What kind of request can somebody make in a dream state? That means that this desire of Solomon has been ingrained deep in his subconscious. He had desired it greatly, such that even in his sleep, he knew exactly what he wanted from God. He did not have to think about it.

Now, if God says to you this day like He is saying to you reading this book, "What do you want so that you can glorify God in your life?" You have only one life. I used to pray this prayer and still do, "*Oh God, I have only one life. And I am determined that I must glorify You with it.*" God is saying to us, "You have only one life, what do you want Me to do for you?" It is vital to seek that anointing that opens up the inner eyes and ears; desire discernment, hearing ears, and seeing eyes.

In a time of drought in Israel, Elijah said to Ahab, "It is time for you to go because there is a sound of abundance of rain." Where did he hear that? There was no rain anywhere, but Elijah said, "I can hear the noise of abundant rainfall." He sent his servant to look, and the servant returned with a report that there was no sign of rain. Yes, in other words, what Elijah heard, had not begun to manifest. However, he was so sure about what he heard that he told his servant seven times to go and check for clouds in the sky. He knew the rain would surely come. The servant returned the seventh time and said, "The cloud is just the size of a clenched fist."

"That's it," Elijah said, and the rain was all over the place in no time. When you hear something in the spiritual realm, you begin to understand how to walk with God to actualize what you have heard here on earth. That's why spiritual intelligence empowers faith, emboldens a man in the exercise of the prophetic calling. "I have seen it," he says, and "that's why I don't take no for an answer, and that's why I firmly believe that it will come through."

It is different when I believe God for something, and I am praying for it. But when I have experienced what God is about, I am mandated to enforce it. That's why trust or faith is natural for people who receive spiritual intelligence; they don't have to struggle to trust God—they have heard it and have seen and touched it. The Bible tells us in chapter one of the Book of Ephesians that *God has given us all the spiritual blessings*, but where did He store them? He stored then in heavenly places. And once we know that these blessings are real, we trust God and pray to bring them down for God's glory on earth as it is in heaven.

Ask the Lord today for the Holy Spirit's power to open your spiritual eyes and ears so that you can enter into a new dimension of spiritual life. But I want to emphasize that this kind of intimacy is only available for people who have truly repented of their sins and have invited the Lord Jesus into their hearts as their Lord and

Saviour. The way to simplify this is to realize that everybody has a throne in their heart on which three can sit and rule: you or the devil and the world or God. There comes a time in a person's life when you clear all usurpers on the throne of your heart and say, "Lord Jesus, come and sit here and rule and reign over my life. It's a decision that transforms us because, from that day onwards, your life becomes a constant waiting for what God wants and for what He wills to accomplish through your life.

The beautiful thing about God is that when a person comes to Him honestly desiring Him and His will, their growth pattern is geometric, and they can go from point one to five because that's God and His favors to those who obey Him. So, if you surrender your life this moment, your inner eyes can be opened. The day I got born again was the day I began to hear God, that very first day. Interestingly, that was how I got born again. I was already leaving the outreach meeting venue when the Holy Spirit whispered to me; He said, *"Go back. That's where you belong."* And since I went back that day on June 28, 1970, I can testify that I have heard that voice ever since, and I have several testimonies to the reality of the voice that speaks to our hearts from heaven – the communion of the Holy Spirit.

When I got to the University of Ibadan in 1970, and I discovered that I wasn't admitted to the Faculty of Medicine, I was shattered, to say the least. But that voice spoke to me. It said, *"You'll study medicine, don't worry. Go and register anywhere you are asked to register."* At the end of my prelim year, they took us over to medicine. You see, the voice is there at every stop to empower you, encourage you, give you faith, strengthen you, make you bold in the face of uncertainties, and keep you strong. That was my experience in that one year that looked interminable as hope hung in the balance.

Besides, the voice is also there to show you the path of humility, kindness, love — all the virtues that are so protective, the little things that you and I need to do to make sure the devil doesn't get into our path of life to frustrate the divine purposes with our cooperation. You and I need that voice. Everyone I dare say needs spiritual intelligence.

One thing to always remember is that God cannot fill a dirty vessel. That is why the Bible says, "Let every man purge himself. Let him that names the name of Christ depart from iniquity." It says, "if any man purges himself, he will be a vessel unto honor." God will empower you. The Holy Spirit will quicken you. You are nowhere that God cannot be or has not been to give you insight and wisdom so you can stay godly in that place. God has a secret monitor inside each of us: it is the spirit He gave to man at creation. The Bible calls it the candle of the LORD that searches our heart always - Proverbs 20:27.

Anyone who ever imagines that he can hide from God is self-deceived.

You and I can be sure that there is no kind of pressure you face that His intelligence proddings cannot keep you godly no matter where you are. If you are determined to be a part of this and want to end the old to begin the new, I want you to pray wherever you are and say: *"Lord Jesus, forgive my sin. Wash away my past. From today, I dethrone all usurpers in my heart, and I invite You to come and sit on the throne of my heart and rule over my life in everything. I will love You, I will serve You, and You will be my Lord and Master all the days of my life. I repent of all my sins. By Your grace, I will not go back to them again, but by the Holy Spirit's power, I will love and serve You till I see You in heaven. Thank You for saving me. In Jesus' name, I pray. Amen."*

Say that prayer with all your heart and God who knows and sees every man's heart, will visit and receive you.

ABOUT THE AUTHOR

Dr. Okey Onuzo is a Consultant Nephrologist and the pioneer physician of the first private dialysis center in Nigeria to treat patients with kidney failure and related conditions. Life Support Medical Centre opened its doors to patients officially on October 4, 1986. He was trained both in Nigeria and the USA.

Dr. Onuzo received the Lord Jesus Christ as his personal Lord and Saviour on June 28, 1970, at a guest invitational service. On the night of June 28, he had a vivid dream where a voice asked him to wake up and read John 6:20. That Scripture reads, "*It is I, be not afraid.*" That was his first encounter with the Lord Jesus Christ. It changed his life entirely and set him on a course to know the One who has called him.

In 1973, at an anointing service at the University of Ibadan in Nigeria, he received an apostolic calling with emphasis on the teaching and the prophetic ministries. He has watched over the years as the Holy Spirit has exposed and expanded these callings to touch several lives in different parts of the world.

Dr. Onuzo has authored several books that try to survey various dimensions of the Spirit-led life. He is generally acknowledged as a conference and seminar speaker, and minister of God's word. Formerly, the Associate Pastor of the National Headquarter Church of the Foursquare Gospel Church in Nigeria; pioneer chapter President of the Full Gospel Business Men's Fellowship International (FGBMFI), Ikeja in 1986 from which he rose to become a National Director of the Fellowship in Nigeria, before stepping aside in the year 2000.

Currently, he serves as the President, Life Link Worldwide Ministries. He runs the Kingdom Life Seminars to raise a community of believers, disciples who desire to follow in the footprints of our Lord Jesus Christ.

He is married to Mariam, a medical doctor, and they have four children: Dilichi, Chinaza, Dinachi, and Chibundu.

BOOKS BY OKEY ONUZO

1. The Convert and the Counsellor

2. Pathway to Conversational Prayers

3. You May Kiss the Bride: Choice, Engagement, Courtship, Marriage, Divorce, Remarriage, Polygamy-- and the Christian

4. Dimensions of Faith

5. Minspi

6. God's Will, The Way to Power

7. You May Kiss the Bride: Choice and Marriage

8. Spiritual Intelligence

9. The Beatitudes: The Spiritual Overhauling Kit

OPERATE IN DIVINE ACCURACY

You don't have to live unaware of the enemy's plans. God has a system in place to keep you a step ahead of the devil. Take advantage of *Spiritual Intelligence* to avert danger, make accurate decisions, and live an all-round victorious life.

In this book, Okey Onuzo through profound teaching of Biblical principles and sharing of life's experiences presents God's provision for your protection and well being.

Printed in Great Britain
by Amazon